MR SMITH'S
VEGETABLE GARDEN

by Geoffrey Smith

Illustrated by Colin Gray

Edited by Brian Davies

BRITISH BROADCASTING CORPORATION

Published to accompany the BBC-tv series Mr Smith's Vegetable Garden produced by Peter Riding and Brian Davies and first broadcast from March 1976.

Published to accompany a series of programmes prepared in consultation with the BBC Further Education Advisory Council.

Other BBC books by the author
Mr Smith's Gardening Book
Mr Smith's Flower Garden
Mr Smith's Fruit Garden
Mr Smith Propagates Plants

The photographs on front and back covers and page 4 were specially taken by Arthur Smith of Rose Productions.

First published 1976
Reprinted 1976 (three times), 1977, 1979 (twice)

Published by the British Broadcasting Corporation, 35 Marylebone High Street, London, W1M 4AA.

Set in 9/10pt Plantin 110 Monophoto
Printed in England by Alan Pooley Printing Limited,
Tunbridge Wells, Kent.
ISBN: 0 563 16010 1

Contents

Introduction

Vegetable growing is not just a short cut to cheaper me though this is a very acceptable bonus. To grow good cr requires a certain amount of physical activity outdoors the fresh air. The act of cultivating the soil provide welcome contrast to the tension of everyday life. Half hour working in the garden leaves one completely relax the well-being of the cabbage crop, for a while, is m important than the state of the pound.

Homegrown vegetables look more appetising, taste be and I am convinced, do me more good than the shop bou article. Anyone can grow beetroot, cabbage or potat even the absolute beginner. Tomatoes, peppers, must and cress will grow and crop well in pots on the kitc window sill. Salads can be cultivated in a window box. get the most out of the garden it is essential to work on soil. The best fertilisers are compost or manure plus sweat of honest toil. Green fingers start with a healthy s

Good luck with the garden.

oils are grouped under three broad headings – sand – loam
clay. All require the same basic cultivation but at different
mes of the year.

ANDY SOILS are made of coarse particles. They should
e dug and dressed with organic matter in JANUARY and
BRUARY. This ensures valuable chemicals are not leached
ut by rain.

AY SOILS have particles so small that water does not pass
rough easily. These should be dug in Autumn so the frost
n break them down. Compost and manure help improve
eir workability.

AM SOILS can vary in structure. They cover the whole
nge between sand and clay. Usually they are easy to work.
hey can be dug whenever conditions permit over Winter,
ing just enough compost or manure to maintain them in a
od physical condition.

ery rough ground is made easier to work if peat and
mpost is worked into it. Rather than spread a little over a
de area, concentrate on say 10 sq. yds. one year to a depth
10 inches and a similar area the next year.

anure improves the texture and fertility of all soils. It also
proves the drainage in heavier soils.

me corrects acidity and improves the workability,
leasing minerals in acid soils. Apply lime to light acid soils
ery 2 years, to clay soils every 3 years. To check the
idity and alkalinity of soil do a simple chemical test with a
oprietary kit. Acidity and alkalinity are expressed as a pH
mber, 7 is neutral, above 7 is alkaline, below 7 is acid.

ils with too much lime may be dressed with farm manure
peat.

ols

rden tools are expensive so buy only the absolute
entials. Buy the best quality the budget allows (not
cessarily the most expensive). Look after them.

ade used for digging, weed control, earthing up.

rk used for digging, lifting root crops, breaking down
gh dug land for sowing, so the air and rain can penetrate
ily.

owel used for planting and transplanting.

rden Line essential to maintain neat straight lines.

ke used for final levelling of soil before seed sowing,
aring up weeds and crop debris, drawing drills.

e used to control weeds and to aerate the soil.

Digging

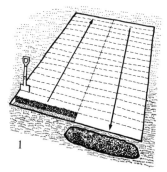

Digging cleans dirty land by improving drainage
aeration. At the same time, by mixing in organic mater
improves the fertility. It is hard work but r[
worthwhile. Always:–

USE a clean sharp spade.

DO NOT try and lift too much earth at a time. Small spad[
remove any risk of back injury.

DO NOT hurry the work; aim at a moderate, metho[
rhythm which will not overtax muscles unaccustome[
heavy digging.

Divide the plot into two halves (1).

For the first trench only, put all the dug out soil ont[
undug half. Work up the first half of the plot then work [
down the second half. Finally use the original soil to f[
the last trench.

The alternative is to take out a trench across the whole [
wheel it in a barrow to the far end so the trench left w[
digging is completed can be filled – a most labor[
business.

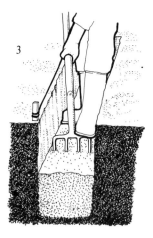

SINGLE TRENCHING means digging out a trench 10 t[
inches deep and the width of a spade (2). Manure ca[
added to the trench bottom before refilling it with soil[

DOUBLE DIGGING means working the soil 20 to 24 in[
deep. Dig over the top 10 inches. Then with a fork brea[
the exposed soil in the trench bottom to a further 10 t[
inches (3). Double trenching is good for cleaning w[
infested land or breaking in pasture land for cropping.[
also advisable for crops like runner beans. Changing [
position of the runner beans on the plot each year ens[
that the whole plot is double dug.

When digging clay soils in the Autumn, leave it in [
lumps, which will be broken down into crumbly piece[
the frost.

When digging sandy soils in the Spring, make sure [
surface is left level. This makes preparation of the seed[
easier.

It is essential that all types of soil should be well drai[
Without this the passage of water is restricted and as a re[
roots die off. Good drainage depends on an open struct[
in the soil. The addition of compost or farmyard mar[
helps. Drainage in clay soils may be helped by adding [
when digging has been completed. This helps to bind [
fine particles together.

Digging without the addition of farmyard manure[
compost to provide humus will lead to a poor, lifeless s[

Composting

armyard manure, peat, or any other organic material
hich will break down, all helps to keep the soil in good
ondition.

armyard manure is one of the best of all soil dressings but
emember it must be well rotted before being dug in. Cow
nanure is good for light soil, and horse manure for heavy
oil. It is possible to over-manure so use only a little and
ften.

Vhen farmyard manure is unobtainable make your own
ompost. Take 4 wooden stakes about 5 feet long and
ammer them into the ground to a depth of 12 to 18 inches
o make a 4 foot square box. Surround the stakes with 3 inch
vide board, spaced 1½ inches apart to let air in, to make 4
ides, 3½ to 4 feet high. Plastic netting will do just as well.

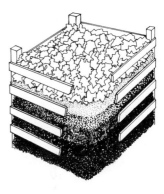

Place all non-wood plant material, lawn cuttings and leaves
nto the box. Air and water are needed to break down the
•lant material. During this process heat is produced which,
n a well-made heap, will kill weeds and diseased spores. DO
OT put any roots onto the compost heap as these can
arbour disease. Starting in the early Summer will ensure a
ood compost heap in the Autumn. If the weather is very
vet cover the heap with wood or polythene to prevent the
naterials becoming waterlogged.

)nly use the well-rotted compost, brown-black, which is
ound at the bottom and middle of the heap. Fork this into
he surface layer (up to 12 inches deep). One or two
padefuls per square yard should be enough. With deep
ooted vegetables like runner beans the compost should be
orked to a depth of 20 inches.

n Summer compost can be used to top dress around plants
mulching) to help retain moisture and prevent roots from
corching. The remains of the compost heap make an ideal
pot to plant marrows, courgettes and cucumbers.

Chemical fertilisers should not be used alone but only to
supplement organic manure. They help to provide the
hree essential elements for healthy plant growth.
NITROGEN – this promotes leaf growth.
SUPERPHOSPHATE – this builds up a strong root system.
POTASH – this gives colour and flavour.

Being a leaf crop, cabbage will respond to fairly heavy
nitrogenous dressing.

Carrots will require both extra superphosphate and potash
to develop large well coloured roots.

Trace elements (e.g. magnesium, boron, iron) are usually
present in a well manured soil in sufficient quantity for most
crop needs.

Rotation

Rotation means not growing the same crop on the sam[e] place each year. This reduces the risk of disease build u[p].

For example, if cabbage, Brussels sprouts and cauliflow[er] (all members of the brassica family) are grown year aft[er] year in the same soil there could be a build up of the disea[se] club root. This can often reduce the crop or even kill th[e] plants.

Another important reason for rotation is to make use [of] fertilizer left over from the previous crop. For exampl[e] follow potatoes with peas. Peas are greedy feeders and th[e] soil has been well manured for the potatoes so they will cr[op] well.

4-Year Rotation Plan

1 Potatoes 2 Peas, beans – dwarf and broad, leek[s,] lettuce 3 Cabbage and Winter greens 4 Carrot[s,] beetroots, turnips, parsnips.

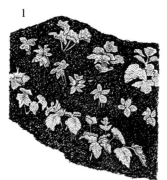

1st Year	1	2	3	4
2nd Year	2	3	4	1
3rd Year	3	4	1	2
4th Year	4	1	2	3
1st Year	1	2	3	4

Permanent crops such as herbs, rhubarb and artichokes d[o] not fit into the rotation and are best planted at the end of th[e] plot or in an odd corner of the garden.

Intercropping

Make use of all the space available by growing rows of quic[k] maturing crops between those which take longer to gro[w.] For example, sow radish with parsnips (1); lettuce betwee[n] rows of peas; marrows between sprouts; spring onions wit[h] lettuce and radish between rows of cabbage.

Catch Cropping

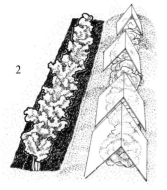

Catch cropping means growing a quick maturing cro[p] whenever any land falls vacant for a short period. Fo[r] example, lettuce can be grown on the ridge of soil from [the] trench dug for celery (2). The lettuce will mature before th[e] soil is needed for earthing up the celery.

Successional Cropping

Successional cropping means providing a continuou[s] supply of different vegetables over as long a period a[s] possible. For example, cabbage or leeks to follow potatoe[s] or early peas in the same bed.

his is a good way to beat the weather and give the crops a
ing start in the Spring. Hardy plants such as onions,
bbages or lettuces can be grown indoors from JANUARY to
rly MARCH and are then planted out under protection
om the weather, usually under cloches. A warm start
doors is advisable for tender plants such as tomatoes,
urgettes, peppers and cucumbers.

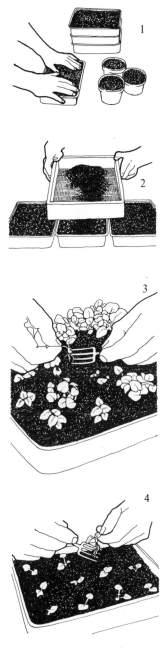

o sow indoors use pots or trays with a layer of broken clay
ot, gravel, or coarse peat along the bottom of the container
  ensure good drainage. Fill with a proprietory SEED
MPOST. A good compost provides moisture, air, and, after
rmination, a supply of food. Any material which does this
ficiently is suitable for seed growing. Warmth is also
cessary. Firm the compost down lightly (1) and then
INLY scatter the seed over it. Fine seed may be mixed
th brick dust or sand to make certain they are spaced
enly. Then cover the seed with a little more compost (2)
d water in. To make certain the compost is evenly moist,
merse the container up to the rim in a bowl of water. Seed
 seedlings must never be short of water. Cover newly
wn seeds with glass and a sheet of newspaper to prevent
e compost drying out – this also helps maintain a steady
mperature and humidity. Keep in a warm place – the
ring cupboard is ideal. When shoots appear, remove the
vers and place in a warm, light, airy position, e.g. a
indow sill.

hen two leaves appear lift the seedlings CAREFULLY by the
af tips (pricking out) taking care not to pinch the stem (3).
n old table fork is ideal. Transfer to pots or trays which
ntain POTTING COMPOST. Make a hole with a blunt ended
iece of wood large enough to hold the roots, then firm the
urrounding compost gently so an even pressure is applied
 bring root and compost into close contact. MAKE CERTAIN
hen pricking out that each seedling is given enough space
 grow without undue competition for light and food (4).

B If you smoke, wash hands before handling tomato plants.
Grow them on in a temperature of 60 degrees F. until
eedlings are ready to plant out. Then by allowing more air
 and reducing the temperature, harden off so that when
oved outdoors there is no check to growth.

ne tip – make sure the potting compost is moist enough
efore use. For a soil based compost a test is to take a
andful and squeeze. If it crumbles when the hand is
pened – too dry; if it stays compacted – too wet; if it cracks
 is just right. For a peat based compost squeeze a handful
ard. If water just oozes out between the fingers then the
mixture is moist enough.

Sowing Outdoors

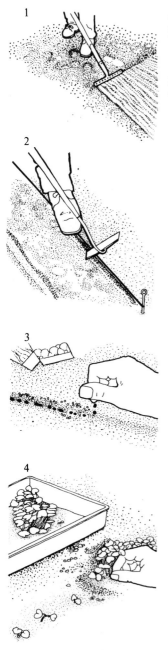

1

2

3

4

A good, crumbly soil is essential for easy sowing and successful germination. Digging the soil well during the Winter should ensure a good tilth, as gardeners say, in the Spring. This means that the tilled soil will rake down in the Spring to a fine level seed bed: no hard lumps of earth, no holes to fill with water after every shower. This is why on a clay soil it is so important to get the digging completed in the Autumn. Over Winter the alternate freezing and thawing breaks up the hard clods. If the soil is still lumpy after Winter digging, then add a little damp peat to the top 3 inches of the surface when raking down in Spring. An alternative method is to add sand or boiler ashes, which have been left to weather.

Freshly dug soil may be firmed by treading along the sowing surface ('the gardener's shuffle') and a final raking down will help to provide ideal sowing conditions (1).

Use the corner of a hoe or the sharpened end of a stick to draw out a shallow drill (groove) using the garden line as a guide (2). Sow the seed thinly and evenly into the drill with the fingers (3) instead of shaking them direct from the packet. This makes it easier to control the spacing. Then 'shuffle' or lightly rake the soil down the line to cover the seed. DO NOT RAKE ACROSS THE LINE as this brings the seed to the surface. Make sure there are no over compacted areas as these tend to harden after rain.

Seed may be scattered over a prepared bed – not a good idea in the vegetable garden as it makes weed control very difficult. Seed sown evenly in drills looks neater, ensures even spacing and any weeds which appear can be spotted and removed easily.

The distance between the rows and depth of sowing depends on the vegetables to be sown. Large seeds such as broad beans may be safely sown 2–3 inches deep. Small seed like carrot never more than $\frac{1}{4}-\frac{1}{2}$ inch deep. A tall growing pea, for example 'Alderman', needs at least 20 inches between the rows, whereas a small lettuce, such as 'Tom Thumb', is quite happy with 8 inches.

Once the seedlings emerge, thin out to the recommended distances (4). This prevents overcrowding and ensures they have the optimum space, light and moisture. Do any thinning when seedlings are small – it is much easier to separate them before the tops become tangled.

DO NOT sow vegetables into a cold soil.

DO NOT rake down a clay soil for a seed bed when the weather is wet.

DO NOT sow too deeply.

Cloches and Frames

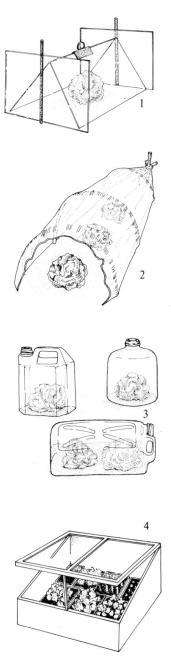

loches enable the gardener to sow early. They protect nder seedlings from bad weather and certain pests. ecause they are intended to encourage growth, make sure e ends are blocked otherwise they act as a wind tunnel.

eas, beans and lettuce may be sown in the Autumn and overed with cloches through the Winter to give early rops. Afterwards the cloches can be moved to Spring sown eeds and then transferred to Summer crops – so they are a ood investment all the year round. Cloches are made of lass, polythene or translucent plastic.

ilass cloches are the best to buy but they can be tricky and angerous to handle. They are available in various shapes nd sizes. The simplest kind is made from two plain sheets f glass in the shape of an inverted V (1). Plastic cloches are lmost as good and are unbreakable.

Another idea is to use clear sheets of polythene or orrugated PVC supported by circular metal frames (2) and blocked at the ends to keep out cold winds. These have the lisadvantage of deteriorating in the ultra-violet rays of unlight and usually have to be renewed every three or four ears. Cheapest of all are large, translucent plastic squash nd detergent bottles. Remove the top, wash them out well, ut off the bottom part and then they will make very effective cloches (3).

Frames

A frame is another useful garden aid. A loose wall of breeze blocks with polythene or an old window frame to cover it will function very well. A better buy is a permanent frame constructed in brick, wood, concrete or metal and covered by a glazed hand light (4). In addition this type can be heated electrically. This means that the frame can be used as a hot bed by running low voltage cables 6 inches below the surface of the soil. Switch the heat on for a few days before planting to pre-warm the soil. Lightweight metal frames are popular and let in more light than the conventional wooden frame, but they have the disadvantage of being colder in the Winter. The cheapest frame is made from four earth walls covered with an old window frame.

To get the maximum benefit out of the frame, cropping should be planned so it is in use most of the year. For example, frames used to overwinter cauliflower plants can then be cropped with cucumber in the Summer and sown with lettuce and spring onions in mid-SEPTEMBER. Carrots and radish sown in DECEMBER and JANUARY will be harvested in mid-MAY in time to plant melons.

11

Artichokes/Asparagus

ARTICHOKES – GLOBE

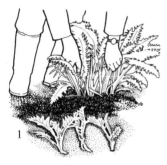

1

How to grow

Plant in APRIL 30 inches apart in well manured, fertile soil i
sheltered position. Use suckers which have been potted u
and overwintered in a cold frame.

To obtain strong plants do not allow them to produce bud
the edible part, in the first year. Feed with liquid manu
and mulch with compost to hold moisture.

To maintain good plants, remove side shoots (1) an
replant every five years as they deteriorate. In cold are
protect with straw during severe weather. No rotatic
necessary – it is a perennial.

Try the variety 'Green and Purple Globe'.

Pests and diseases

Usually no problems.

Storage and kitchen hints

To freeze, remove outer leaves and stalks. Trim tops an
stems. Wash in cold water, blanch a few at a time for 8–1
minutes. Cool and drain upside-down. Pack in a stron
plastic container.

ASPARAGUS

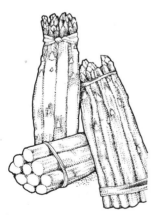

How to grow

Asparagus beds occupy the land permanently, only crop
ping for 5–6 weeks but the unique flavour makes this an
attractive early Summer vegetable.

A perennial plant, it needs a light, well drained soil which
must be dug over well the previous Autumn. Heavy soil
should be worked 15 inches deep and the general level of the
bed raised slightly to improve the drainage with plenty o
manure or compost added to the top 10 inches on light soils
Add 2 oz of bone meal per sq. yd. before planting the
crowns (roots).

Sow seeds in APRIL in shallow drills and 9 inches apart
Thin seedlings to 12 inches apart when 3–4 inches high
Water well in dry weather and keep weed free.

Cut feather-like leaves down to soil level in the Autumn. In
the Spring lift the roots carefully and plant 18 inches apart
in the bed with their crowns 4 inches below the surface.
Shoots from these may be cut in the second year after
planting.

You can save time and effort by buying two-year old crowns
and they will produce the year after planting. Cut asparagus
from 2–3 year old crowns when growths are 4–6 inches

ove soil from MAY to mid-JUNE. Cut about 4 inches below
surface and go over bed twice a week. Stop cutting in mid-
JUNE so the remaining stems can build up strong crowns for
the following Spring. Every Autumn, cut back to an inch
above soil level and mulch with well-rotted manure or
compost to ensure a good supply of shoots next year.

Try the variety 'Martha Washington'.

Pests and diseases

Asparagus beetles feed on young stems and leaves. Spray
with liquid derris.

Root rot – difficult to detect as there are no external
symptoms until too late. Usually associated with bad
drainage. It is caused by fungi and results in sickly looking
plants which eventually wilt and die.

Storage and kitchen hints

For freezing, sort into thick and thin stems. Wash in cold
water and blanch thin stems for 2 minutes and thick stems
for 4 minutes. Tie into small bunches and separate by thin
strips of polythene to prevent sticking together. Cook stems
in an asparagus ring and serve with melted butter.

AUBERGINES

How to grow

Sow in APRIL under glass – two to a peat pot. Remove
weakest after germination. Once two leaves unfurl, they can
be hardened off and put outdoors in late MAY in the South.
Elsewhere, protection by glass or polythene is required.
They can be grown in peat filled polythene bags or as a pot
plant.

When 6–9 inches high, pinch out the top. Tap plants daily
and syringe over to help pollination. When 4 fruits have
formed, pinch out side growths. Liquid feed every 7–10
days once fruit has formed.

Try the variety 'Early Long Purple'.

Pest and diseases

Red spider – syringe with water in dry weather.

Storage and kitchen hints

Peel the fruit and cut into inch-thick slices. Blanch for 4
minutes, chill and dry. Pack in layers of 4 or 5 slices, each
separated by a thin piece of polythene to prevent sticking.
Try lightly fried with courgettes in olive oil.

Beans – Broad

1

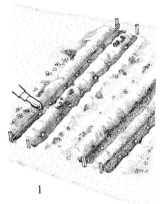

2

How to grow

Broad beans do best on well manured ground which hold moisture and usually follow potatoes in the crop rotation. dressing of fertilizer (2 oz per sq. yd.) is recommended 1 days before sowing.

The seeds can be sown in FEBRUARY in a sheltered plac elsewhere MARCH to APRIL. Sow in double rows 6–9 inche apart in a shallow trench 3 inches deep with 2 feet betwee each double row (1). Alternatively, in single rows, 18 inche apart by 3 inches deep with 6–9 inches between the seed Sow additional rows until MAY for picking in late Summe. They can be sown in the Autumn to overwinter and give a early crop.

On a wind-swept site support with canes or string as the can grow to 4 feet 6 inches in height.

You can save your own seed, if the variety is a good one, b letting the pods ripen on the plant (turn black). Then pu up the whole plant, hang upside down over a sheet of pape. The ripe beans just drop off; store in a cool dry place.

When picking has finished, dig the whole of the plant int the soil as green manure and use the site for next year' cabbages.

Try the varieties 'Imperial White' and 'Greensleeves'.

The variety 'Meteor' yields a large crop of medium lengt pods, and these beans are ideal for freezing.

Pests and diseases

Blackfly – to prevent, remove the growing tip as the lowe pods set (2). Spray with liquid derris.

Chocolate spot – brown spots on leaves which can be avoide by a well drained soil.

Young plants can be attacked by *weevils* which eat piece out of the leaves. These can be controlled by derris dust.

Storage and kitchen hints

For the best results, pick broad beans while young – blacl scars on beans show they are getting old. For freezing, wasl well and blanch for 3 minutes. When cooled, drain and pacl in polythene bags.

Broad beans are delicious served with fried bacon and nev potatoes.

When fresh vegetables are scarce, try cooking the tips o broad beans and the immature pods. Eat like spinach. Har broad beans may be used for making soup.

Beans – Dwarf French

ow to grow

hese follow potatoes in the rotation so the land is already
eply worked and well manured. Fork in 2 oz per sq. yd. of
balanced fertilizer 10 days before sowing.

ow in early MAY in the South, a fortnight later in the
orth, in rows up to 18 inches apart, 1½ inches deep with
eds 4 inches apart in the rows. Thin to 8 inches apart if all
rminate. Space the rows 12 inches apart on exposed sites
d thin seedlings to six inches apart. The plants then
pport each other. On a wind-swept site support with
igs as the pods are heavy.

ater and keep the plants weed free, then as the flowers set,
quid feed at 10-day intervals. The plants grow to a height
f 15–18 inches and pods should be picked while still
oung. This helps the plants to carry on cropping for a long
eriod so it is worth going over the bed every second day.
ike other members of the legume family, they put
itrogen back into the soil, so follow with brassicas (e.g.
abbage) which are nitrogen absorbers.

loches are an invaluable garden aid in growing this
egetable. They are used to prewarm the soil. Place the
loches in position 7–10 days before sowing. After sowing,
ave the cloches in place until the plants are touching the
lass.

ry the varieties 'The Prince' and 'Tendergreen'.

ests and diseases

nthracnose (dark sunken patches on pods) – caused by
owing into a cold, wet soil. Control by spraying with
ordeaux mixture.

lalo blight (brown patches on foliage) – burn infected
lants.

rey mould (grey powdery substance on stems and foliage)
thrives on dead vegetables, so clear garden debris.

row resistant varieties like 'The Prince' and do not store
eed from infected plants. Do not plant in the same soil for 4
ears.

torage and kitchen hints

deal for freezing. Select young beans, wash well, trim ends
nd blanch for 3 minutes. Then cool, drain and pack into
olythene bags. They can be bottled by covering layers of
liced beans with salt. (1 lb kitchen salt to 3 lbs beans).

ry them cooked whole, lightly peppered and served cold
ith chicken or turkey salad.

**BEANS –
DWARF FRENCH**

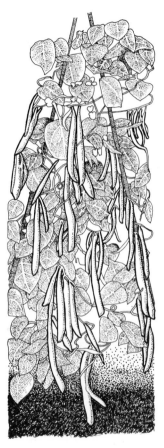

15

Beans – Runner

How to grow

These are the most economical of all Summer crops. T
soil should be double dug the previous Autumn to a de
of 20–24 inches and well manured to help hold moistu
They may be grown across one end or down the edge of
vegetable garden so as to provide shelter for other pla
like tomatoes or sweet corn.

The seed for early crops can be sown in APRIL under cloc
or in the greenhouse in peat pots. They may be grown fr
seed, outdoors, from mid-MAY until late JUNE, spacing
seeds 6 inches apart, 3 inches deep, to be thinned later to
inches.

Plants may be grown up 8-foot canes or poles, or throu
nets or wigwams made by tying several poles together.

'Pinching' out the tips of growing shoots once plants are
inches high will produce an early crop, but then unstopp
plants will outgrow them. Water and syringe in d
weather. Keep the plants well picked over, so no pods
seed. Liquid feeding at regular intervals will keep plants
full crop for several months. Move runner beans each ye
so as to double dig the whole plot in four years. They al
make excellent patio plants because of the brilliant, scar
flowers.

Try the varieties 'Sunset' (early); 'Achievement', 'Strea
line' (maincrop).

Pests and diseases

Blackfly – dust with nicotine or, better, spray with liqu
derris.

Whitefly – a problem in hot weather; spray over with wa
at dusk.

Slugs – put slug pellets down in heaps along the row.

Millepedes – problem in cold, wet weather or weed-ridd
garden. Trap by burying pieces of carrots or potatoes ju
beneath the surface. The pest feeds on these and the who
may be dug up and burnt.

Storage and kitchen hints

For freezing, select young beans, wash well, slice thick
and blanch for 1½–2 minutes. Cool, drain and pack in
polythene bag. Runner beans can be preserved by bottlir
in dry salt. (1 lb kitchen salt to 3 lbs beans).

When pods are young and tender, skin, chop into slices, ar
use in green salads. Alternatively try them served in melte
butter with roast chicken.

Beetroot

How to grow

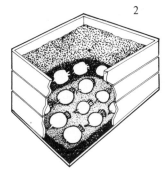

Beetroot MUST NOT be grown in freshly manured land as this produces misshapen roots. It follows cabbage in the rotation.

Fork into the soil a dressing of fertilizer with a high proportion of superphosphate, or apply basic slag (contains phosphate and lime) in the Autumn prior to sowing.

Sow the seeds in shallow drills, 12 inches apart and 1 inch deep during APRIL for early salads. Sow in MAY and JUNE to give a succession and also to provide roots for storing. When seedlings come up they can be thinned to 4 inches to allow room for development. Do not transplant thinnings as they will not grow on and if they do they usually run straight up to seed.

Try the varieties 'Boltardy' or 'Early Bunch' (earlies); the long-rooted 'Cheltenham Green Top' or 'Globe' (main-crop).

Pests and diseases

Usually, nothing to worry about, but *violet root* can be a problem. Difficult to control and covers the roots with purple, web-like strands.

Storage and kitchen hints

Beetroot should be picked while the roots are still tender. Test by cutting in half; the texture should be even with no rings. Start using roots of 'Globe' varieties when they reach the size of a golf ball.

Lift roots for storing with a fork before they harden or get frozen. Twist, DO NOT CUT off the tops (1). Shake the roots clear of soil then store between layers of sand or peat in a frost-free place (2). In milder regions roots may be protected with straw and left in the ground until required. Only store sound roots and check for rot during Winter.

To pickle, wash the roots carefully, cook in boiling salted water (1 oz salt/1 pt water) until tender (1½–2 hours). Skin and cut into thin slices. Pack into jars and immerse in spiced vinegar.

When freezing choose small beets.

Blanching time for small beets – 10 minutes; for large beets cook until tender for about 40–50 minutes. Small beets may be frozen whole, large ones should be sliced. Don't store for too long as they tend to go rubbery.

Try them boiled, hollowed out then filled with chopped green onion, cheese and egg.

BEETROOT

Broccoli (Sprouting)

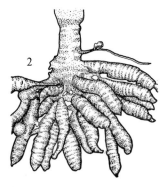

How to grow

Member of the brassica family, others include cabbages Brussels sprouts, cauliflowers, kales, savoys, swedes and turnips.

Broccoli succeed best on firm soils which are well drained 'heavyish' loams well manured for a previous crop of early salads, peas or leeks. A dressing of equal parts super phosphate and sulphate of potash at 2 oz/sq. yd. should be worked into the land a few days before planting.

The seed is sown into the prepared bed during late APRIL to MAY. When the seedlings are large enough to handle, space them out 20 inches apart and 24 inches between rows. Keep the weeds down with a hoe and give heavy waterings during dry weather. No supplementary feeding is required as the broccoli needs to be hardy to stand the Winter. The broccoli spears are ready from FEBRUARY TO MAY.

When harvesting, pick the centre broccoli spears first to encourage side shoots which prolongs cropping.

Try the varieties 'White Sprouting', 'Purple Sprouting' and 'Autumn Spear'. An excellent variety for freezing is 'Express Corona' (F_1 Hybrid). Cut the centre head to allow side shoots to develop. Crops very heavily from AUGUST to SEPTEMBER.

Pests and diseases

Cabbage root fly affects all the brassicas. It is present if a wilting plant, when pulled up in Summer, shows white maggots on the roots (1). Bromophos helps kill them. Try using a tarred disc as a preventive (see page 19).

Club root – symptoms are poor growth and knotted roots (2). Dipping the roots of young plants in calomel paste when transplanting is the usual control.

Storage and kitchen hints

For freezing, select only the youngest spears. Wash well in salt water and shake dry. Blanch for 3–5 minutes (depending on stem thickness), cool and drain. Pack in cartons, stalks to tips.

It really is a must in the garden as it bridges the gap between Winter and Summer vegetables. It crops from FEBRUARY to MAY and the return per plant makes it one of the most economical to grow. Fresh broccoli spears are unobtainable because they do not travel well and are best when picked straight from the plant into the pan.

Cook broccoli spears like asparagus with melted butter.

Brussels Sprouts

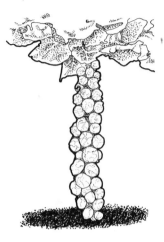

How to grow

Sprouts need firm ground which HAS NOT been freshly manured. Dress the plot with 1½ oz superphosphate and 1 oz sulphate of potash/sq. yd. 14 days before planting.

Sow the seeds in beds MARCH to APRIL and transplant to the prepared plot in late MAY to JUNE, spacing them 24 inches apart and 24 inches between rows. They can be inter-cropped with rows of lettuce (1).

Water well in dry weather and after transplanting.

Pick sprouts as they mature from base upwards. Take dead leaves off plant and leave on the ground to work as a mulch (a top dressing of organic material) or remove to the compost heap. When the sprouts have finished growing, pinch out the top of the plant. Do not waste this as it can be cooked like cabbage.

Try the varieties 'Pier Gynt' and 'Market Rearguard'.

Pests and diseases

All are common to brassicas – cabbages, cauliflowers, Brussels sprouts.

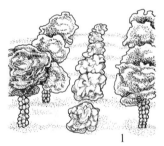

Cabbage root fly – first indication of this is the plant wilting due to white maggots feeding on the roots. Put a tarred felt disc around the stem (2) at planting time to prevent the adult fly laying their eggs. Alternatively dip the roots of young plants in a proprietary dust or paste based on calomel.

Flea beetles – these eat the leaves of seedlings. Combat by watering freely each evening at dusk.

Caterpillars – these defoliate the plants. Remove by hand picking or spraying with liquid derris.

Club root – this deforms the roots. Lime the soil heavily 6–8 oz/sq. yd. Ensure the soil is well drained and dip the roots of young plants in a paste of 4% calomel immediately before planting. As this disease overwinters in the soil, never plant any brassica in the same part of the garden more than once in four years.

Aphids and Whitefly – use malathion dust immediately.

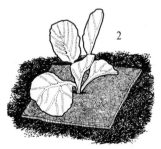

Storage and kitchen hints

For freezing, use small, hard sprouts. Take off the outer leaves and wash well. Blanch for 3–4 minutes (depending on sprout size), cool and drain before packing in polythene bags. Cook by dropping heads into a saucepan of boiling water for 3 minutes – that way they remain firm and do not cook all soggy and yellow.

Cabbage

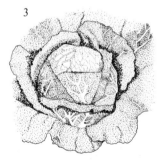

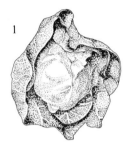

How to grow

Cabbage – Spring (1): A deeply worked, well drained site essential for this overwintering crop. The soil should not b too rich so the site used for early peas will do. Fork in complete fertilizer dressing based on fish meal immediatel the peas are cleared.

Sow the seeds in a nursery bed during late JULY in th North, early AUGUST in the South, to give plants larg enough to plant out in mid-SEPTEMBER – 15 inches betwee the rows, 9 inches between the plants.

In the Spring when the soil warms up dress with a quicl acting nitrogenous fertilizer.

Cut every other plant as Spring greens and leave the rest t heart up.

Try the varieties 'Durham Early' and 'Offenham'.

Cabbage – Summer (2): Plant in land which carried la peas the previous year. Work in a little compost plus general fertilizer at 2 oz/sq. yd.

The seed is sown in MARCH to APRIL in a nursery bed or frame. Plant out during MAY to JUNE 15 inches apart and 1 inches between rows. The plants must be watere thoroughly in dry weather.

Try the varieties 'Winnigstadt', 'Golden Acre' an 'Cannonball'.

Cabbage – Winter and Savoy (3): These follow early salad in the rotation. The soil should be well drained but not rich Fork in a fertilizer dressing of equal parts of super phosphate and potash – 2 oz/sq. yd. Sow in MAY and plan out in JULY 18 inches between rows.

Try the varieties 'Celtic Cross' and 'January King'.

Pests and diseases

Cabbage root fly – white maggots on roots. Put a tarred dis around the stem at planting time to prevent adult fly layin eggs. Dip roots in a proprietary dust or paste based o calomel (see pages 18 and 19).

Club root – deformed roots. Lime soil well 6–8 oz per sq. y and dip roots in paste based on calomel.

For others see Brussels sprouts (page 19)

Storage and kitchen hints

For freezing, only use young, crisp cabbage leaves. Wasl well and cut up finely. Blanch for 1½ minutes, drain an pack small amounts into polythene bags.

Carrots

How to grow

DO NOT SOW in freshly manured land as this causes misshapen roots. Choose a site that has been well manured for a previous crop.

Sow in drills ½-inch deep and 10 inches apart from MARCH onwards. Sow thinly, as carrots which have to be thinned are more prone to attack by carrot root fly.

They do best in sandy soil. Heavy ground should be worked at least 12 inches deep and left in rough clods to weather. Add fertilizer 10 days before seed sowing – 2 oz superphosphate, 1 oz sulphate of potash per sq. yd. To sow in heavy ground, draw drills 3 inches deep, fill with sand and sow into that. They should be thinned to 3 inches apart if roots are for storing.

When hoeing between the rows, work the soil up to the carrots so as to avoid 'Green Shoulders'.

Try the varieties 'Parisian Rondo' (1), 'Amsterdam Forcing' (2), 'Early Nantes' (3) (earlies); 'New Red Intermediate' (4), 'Autumn King' (5), 'Chantenay Red Cored' (6) (all maincrop).

Pests and diseases

Carrot root fly (7) – the first sign is a bronzing of the green leaves. To lessen the risk of carrot fly infestation, dust the rows with soot or grow a row of onions between every three rows of carrots. The smell of the onions disguises that of the carrots. If seedlings have to be thinned then do it in wet weather. This lessens the risk of an attack. Carrot root fly can overwinter in the soil so sow in a different part of garden which has not grown carrots for 4 years.

Wireworms riddle the carrot roots with holes – only a problem on new broken grassland.

Carrot splitting may be caused by sudden rain after a dry spell or by an excess of a nitrogenous dressing – water well in dry weather.

Soft rot occurs in stored roots. Do not store damaged roots and burn those which are infected.

Storage and kitchen hints

Lift roots in OCTOBER. Twist off tops and pack in layers of sand in a box (8). Keep in a frost-proofed shed.

For freezing use only finger-sized roots, not large ones. Scrape, clean and blanch for 3–5 minutes; then cool, drain and pack. Try carrots raw in a salad or cooked lightly and served with melted butter.

CARROTS

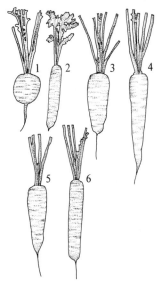

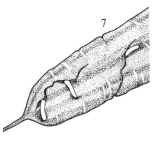

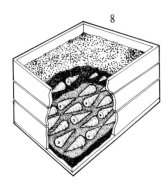

Cauliflower

CAULIFLOWER

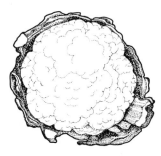

How to grow

These need a rich, well manured, moisture retentive soil s
there is no check to growth which can cause 'Button Heart
(mini-cauliflower instead of a large one). A dressing of fis
meal, approximately 3 oz/sq. yd. before planting, w
improve growth.

Sow the seed under glass from JANUARY to MARCH, c
outdoors APRIL to MAY. This gives a succession of curds fc
the table from early SEPTEMBER to late OCTOBER.

Plant out 18 inches apart, 18 inches between rows, or 2
inches apart, 24 inches between rows for the Autum
varieties.

Keep well watered, liquid feed twice to promote rapi
growth, hoe regularly. A few outer leaves bent over th
hearts will give protection against frost, or in the case c
Summer varieties, excess sun (1).

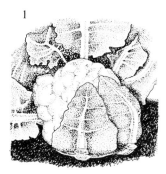

Try the varieties 'All The Year Round', 'Alpha Polaris
'Snowball' (all Summer); 'Kangaroo', 'Autumn Giant
'Superlative Protecting' (all Autumn).

Winter Cauliflower (2): Cultivation is the same as Brocco
(Sprouting) (see page 18). Earth up overwintering plants a
they grow to prevent damage by strong winds.

Try the varieties 'Superb Early White', 'White Cliffs' an
'May Queen'.

Pest and diseases

Like all brassicas (members of the cabbage family) the tw
main problems are *cabbage root fly* – white maggots on th
roots and *club root* – deformed roots.

To prevent the fly laying eggs put a tarred disc around ster
when planting or dip roots in a paste based on calomel.

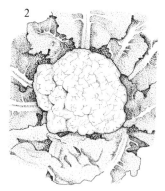

Club root may be checked by liming the soil well 6–8 oz/sc
yd. and dipping the roots in a paste based on calomel. Neve
plant brassicas in the same soil more than once in every
years. Keep down weeds like shepherd's purse as th
disease can overwinter on this.

Cabbage moth – green or brown caterpillars feed on th
leaves and can strip the plant completely. Dust with derri
and pay particular attention to the underside of leaves.

Storage and kitchen hints

For freezing, choose firm compact heads. Wash and brea
into small pieces of about 3 inches in diameter. Add lemo
juice to blanching water to keep heads white. Blanch for
minutes, cool, drain and pack in polythene bags.

Celery

How to grow

Two types: non self-blanching (which needs earthing up) and self-blanching (which needs no earthing up). Both grow well on a peaty soil which holds the moisture.

For the non self-blanching variety, take a trench out 18 inches wide and one spade blade deep. Fork well-rotted manure or compost into the trench bottom, then replace all but the last 3 inches of top soil.

Seeds are sown during MARCH under glass, pricked off into boxes and then hardened off for planting out in the trench in late MAY. 12 inches between plants in the row and 10 inches between rows.

Celery needs constant moisture, so water heavily in dry weather. When non self-blanching plants are 8 inches high, tie the stems up loosely (1). Remove sucker growths which appear from the base of the stems, put on a collar of corrugated paper (2) and earth up with about 3 inches of soil to begin with. Repeat the earthing up at 3-weekly intervals until the soil is up to the leaf base (3). During sharp frost, cover the bed with bracken or straw.

Try the varieties 'Unrivalled' (pink) or 'Solid' (white).

The self-blanching celery does not require trenching or earthing up but still needs a well manured soil. Plant self-blanching celery close together as this helps the plants to support each other.

Try the varieties 'Golden Self Blanch' or 'American Green'.

Pests and diseases

Light brown holes in the leaves means *celery fly* – control by dusting with malathion at the first sign.

Leaf miner – white marks on leaves. It may be checked by hand picking. In a bad attack spray with malathion.

Celery leaf spot – nowadays nearly all the seed is treated against this, but if necessary spray with Bordeaux mixture.

Storage and kitchen hints

Use straight from the ground as required – a slight frost improves the flavour.

For freezing, trim the stalks and wash well. Cut into 1 inch lengths and blanch for 3 minutes. Cool, drain and pack – but these can only be used in cooked dishes.

Try fresh celery soup – it's made with celery, onions, milk, and can be thickened with a little cooked potato – excellent on a cold day.

CELERY

Chicory

CHICORY

1

How to grow

This requires a fertile soil, so follows a crop like potatoes. Fork in a dressing of fish meal, 2 oz/sq. yd. before sowing.

Sow direct in early MAY in drills with 18 inches between the drills. Then thin seedlings to 8 inches apart, so the roots become fully developed.

They can be forced in the open by cutting off the tops 1 inch above the roots and drawing the soil from either side to form a 9-inch ridge over the plants (earthing up). The white chicons (edible part) will eventually push up through the mounds of soil.

Alternatively, lift roots in NOVEMBER and clean. Cut leaves and trim the bottom part of root. Pot up 6-inch long roots, three to a pot, and cover with another pot making sure the drainage hole is blocked as they must be kept in the dark (1). Every root will produce its own 4- to 5-inch long chicon. If the roots are forced in too high a temperature (above 60 degree F) the leaves of the chicons tend to be loose instead of being a tight head and are bitter in taste.

A reliable variety is 'Witloof of Brussels'. This forces better if exposed to frost for a few days.

There is a new cultivated salad variety 'Sugar Loaf' which I tried for the first time this year. During the Summer, the leaves, unlike those of 'Witloof', can be used in salads as a change from lettuce. Sow the seed from JUNE to JULY in rows 15 inches apart. Thin seedlings to 12 inches between plants. The head develops in the same way as 'Cos' lettuce.

Another well-tried variety is 'Red Verona'. Sow the seed from MAY to mid-AUGUST. This gives large, green leaves with a little red colouring, and when forced produces a compact, red head.

Pests and diseases

Usually no problems, but can be subject to attack from *greenfly* which infest lettuce. Spray with liquid derris.

Storage and kitchen hints

Roots should be lifted as required for forcing from the open ground. Seeds sown in MAY will be ready for forcing in NOVEMBER to MARCH.

To free the ground for digging, the roots can be lifted and stored in boxes filled with sand in a cool place (see page 21). Alternatively, heel in (lay in trenches) outdoors on the North side of the plot.

Try raw, crisp chicons with cheese, onion and cold beef.

Courgettes and Marrows

How to grow

Courgettes are mini-marrows and require the same cultivation. They will crop very well if planted out on a stack of old manure or on the remains of last year's compost heap. If planted in soil, enrich with a forkful of rotted manure placed under each plant.

Sow 2 seeds in a peat pot under glass in the third week of APRIL. Thin seedlings to leave the strongest plant to grow on for planting out in early JUNE. The seed may be sown direct, but these plants will crop later – so cover with cloches or inverted jam jars to start with. Keep weed free and well watered. Transferring the pollen from the male flower to female flower (the one with the young fruit behind it) helps the fruit to set (1). A side dressing of nitrogen will help swell the young fruits. Support marrows on a piece of glass to prevent rotting (2). Cut the fruits while still young as this keeps the plant in cropping.

Courgettes can be grown in a polythene bag filled with peat plus fertilizer. They can also be grown as an intercrop between Brussels sprouts. The shady moist conditions provided by the foliage makes an ideal climate. Take care to ensure that the sprouts are not forced into soft growth by too rich a soil.

Try the varieties (courgettes) 'Golden Zucchini' and 'True French'.

Try the varieties (marrow) 'Tender and True' and 'Green Bush Improved'.

Pests and diseases

Slugs cleared by hand picking after dark by torchlight.

Stem rot caused by water resting at base of stem – so plant in a slight mound, or plunge a plastic or clay pot into the compost near the plant and water into that.

Storage and kitchen hints

Marrows and courgettes must be picked before the cold weather sets in. They can be stored in net bags or old nylon tights and hung up in a frost free place – a spare bedroom is ideal. Make sure that the fruits do not touch each other as this can cause rot to set in.

They can be frozen successfully. Slice young fruits and blanch for 2 minutes. Cool, drain and place a thin piece of polythene between slices to prevent them sticking together.

Try them fried in slices with bacon or stuffed with chopped ham and garlic.

COURGETTES AND MARROWS

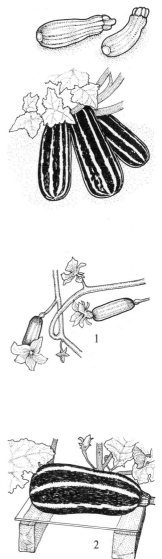

1

2

Cucumbers

CUCUMBERS

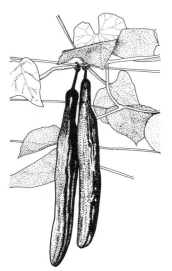

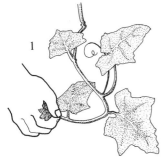

1

How to grow

Prepare suitable beds in a greenhouse or frame with mixture of 2 parts garden soil and 1 part manure compost, plus a 5-inch pot of John Innes base fertilizer fish meal to each barrow load.

Sow the seeds singly in pots during APRIL and place over warm radiator or in a greenhouse. After germination mov to a light position and plant out when the first pair of tru leaves are fully open. 2 plants can be grown in a 3-foot pea compost bag or 1 plant in a large pot. Syringe over dail with water. Never allow the plants to dry out. Top dres after first fruits are cut with mixture of soil and fertilize DO NOT overfeed with nitrogen as this may cause bitte fruits.

The growing point can be removed when the main stem 24–30 inches in length. Stop the side growths (fru bearing) after the second leaf has formed (1). An subsequent side growths are stopped after one leaf. Th keeps the plant in full fruit production. All tendrils (thi curling outgrowth from the stem) and male flowers shoul also be removed.

During the very hot, sunny weather keep the plants shade by whitewashing the glass of frames or greenhous Alternatively use covers made from netting or builder laths which can be removed in dull weather. Cut fruits they mature. Thin overcrowded shoots and foliage.

Try the varieties 'Butchers Disease Resisting', 'Tempes (all female flowers); 'Burpless Tasty Green' (outdoor).

Pests and diseases

Red spider causes leaves to lose colour. To deter this pes syringe the leaves at midday to provide damp conditions

Canker can be caused by too wet a soil – reduce wate Withering of fruits can mean poor soil conditions.

Leaf spot – causes leaves to turn brown and the plant to di Maintain strict garden hygiene.

Wilting – indicates that the plant is diseased. Usual caused by a root disease – fusarium.

Storage and kitchen hints

Usually eaten as a salad vegetable but it can be cooked. Pee cut in half lengthwise and dice. Cook gently in butter for u to 20 minutes and serve with white sauce.

Cucumbers mixed in a blender with carrot and lemon juic make a very palatable cooling drink.

Herbs

Herbs are only needed in limited quantities and are best grown in a corner near the house. They require a well prepared, freely drained soil. Herbs for storing should always be harvested when the weather is fine. They should be dried thoroughly before storing.

As well as adding flavour to cooking they can be used amongst the linen and elsewhere to give fragrance. Rosemary is frequently used as a hair rinse.

Basil (1)

This annual grows in a well drained, light soil and needs a sheltered place. Seeds may be sown in MAY and leaves harvested in AUGUST to OCTOBER or before if they are to be dried. Can be used for flavouring in salads, tomatoes, soups, sauces and omelettes.

Bay (2)

Prefers a slightly lime soil and is usually bought as a pot-grown plant. In most areas it needs a sheltered corner against a house wall. Bay makes a good tub plant and can then be given protection in severe weather. A useful ornamental evergreen which will tolerate clipping.

Place 1 or 2 leaves inside a grayling before cooking with bacon. Also used in a Bouquet Garni.

Chervil (3)

Plant in a shady position. This annual, with fern-like leaves is used to flavour soups and salads. Pick leaves 7–9 weeks after sowing in the first year and before flowering in the second. Used to flavour salads, soups and sauces.

Chives (4)

The soil should be manured and well dug the previous Autumn. They can be bought from a nursery and planted in MARCH 6 inches apart. Trim the plants over regularly to provide juicy young growths.

Use for salads in the Spring. Cook with old potatoes to make them more appetising, or chop into soured cream and serve with potatoes in their jackets.

Dill (5)

Sow the seeds in a well drained soil and in a sunny position. Dill grows to a height of 3 feet and spreads to 2 feet. It is an annual with fine bluish-green leaves and yellow flowers. Leaves should be picked before seeds set. Use dried leaves for flavouring beans and poultry, and the seed in pickles.

HERBS

Herbs

Garlic (1)

The soil should be manured and dug the previous Autumn. Like onions they grow best in a rich soil. The bulbs can be bought from a greengrocer. They are a mass of individual leaves known as cloves. These cloves should be separated and planted in a sunny position 1 inch deep and 9 inches apart immediately the weather becomes warm in the Spring. Flower heads which develop should be pinched out as soon as they show. When foilage yellows, the bulbs are lifted and dried thoroughly before storing in a dry, frost-free place.

Try rubbing a clove round a salad bowl to give the salad that extra flavour, or insert a crushed clove in roast pork.

Mint (2)

Mint spreads so quickly that it is best grown in a restricted space, either in a bucket with holes in the bottom plunged in the garden or in a narrow border by a path. It enjoys a moist soil in partial shade and is grown from root runners. Plant in early MARCH, keep weed free and top dress with well rotted compost.

Mint can be forced by lifting strong roots, planting them in boxes then taking them onto a warm window ledge or into a greenhouse. Stems may be cut and dried in early JULY for Winter use. Try chopped mint with minced mutton – it makes a tasty filling for a pasty.

Parsley (3)

Sow 1 inch apart in short 4 foot rows in the Spring. It is slow to germinate, so use radish as an indicator. Boiling water poured into the drill before sowing quickens germination. Thin seedlings to 6 inches apart when large enough. Another sowing may be made in JULY. Cut leaves before the plant flowers and use them as a garnish or flavouring.

Adds a piquancy to celery soup and to white sauce. Good varieties are 'Claudia' and 'Green Velvet'.

Pot Marjoram (4)

This needs a light, fertile soil and a good sunny position. It may be grown from seed, sown under glass in MARCH and planted out in late APRIL – 9 inches apart. Probably better to buy from a nursery. The plants should be clipped to remove flowerbuds. Cut the sprigs on a bright sunny day and dry in a low oven or a light airy shed.

Try in omelettes or sprinkled on vegetable soup.

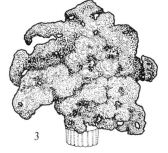

Rosemary (1)

A shrub attractive enough to warrant a select place beside the housewall. It grows 5 feet high, evergreen with blue flowers. Needs a light, well drained soil. Plant from a nursery in APRIL-MAY. Mulch each year with well-rotted compost in the Spring. Use with meat and poultry.

Sage (2)

Another shrub worthy of a select place in the shrub border if the space is limited. It grows 2 foot high with grey green foliage. It requires a light, well drained soil and is best planted in early APRIL. Sage prefers a hot and dry position. Plants may be bought from a nursery, grown from seed or propagated by cuttings from young wood taken in JUNE into a sand frame. Trim plants over regularly to ensure good healthy young shoots – a light dressing of fertilizer in APRIL will encourage strong young growth. Shoots for storing should be pulled on a dry day in JULY and hung up in a dry, airy shed. Main use is for flavouring stuffing.

Tarragon (3)

A light, well drained soil is essential. Plant roots in MARCH from a nursery or sow seed in APRIL spaced 12 to 15 inches apart. Pinch out the flowering shoots to encourage young, leafy stems – ideal for use in a kitchen. A few young plants grown in a frame will provide a supply of fresh shoots over the Winter.

Tarragon adds a special flavour to cheese and tomato omelette and is best known in Tarragon vinegar used for making mayonnaise sauce.

Thyme (4)

Sow the seed in shallow drills or buy in plants from a nursery. Space 8 inches apart. Top dress the soil in MARCH with powdered sea weed fertilizer. Every third year the old plants should be lifted and divided, replanting the youngest healthy portions to continue the cropping. Like the other herbs, it should not be allowed to flower. Cut the short stems during Summer, dry them in a low oven or a cool, airy place. Rub into flakes and store in a screw top jar.

Lemon thyme is evergreen, which saves drying for Winter use.

Thyme is an essential ingredient for a Bouquet Garni together with parsley, top leaves of celery, a bayleaf and sage all wrapped in a muslin bag. Also used as a herbal seasoning for stock, stews and soups.

Kale/Kohl Rabi

KALE

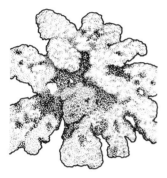

How to grow

A strongly flavoured vegetable whose taste is improved by the frost. Can be grown in the coldest parts and so is very useful in the more exposed gardens. It needs a deeply worked soil, firm but not over rich. The bed which carried early potatoes or peas will be ideal.

Sow the seed in APRIL to MÀY in trays or direct into the open ground. When seedlings are ready, transplant to the cropping area and space 18 inches apart and 24 inches between the rows.

Water well in dry weather. Kale heads are ready for use from late DECEMBER onwards. Cut the heads first as this encourages additional tender side shoots.

Try the variety 'Dwarf Green Curled'.

Pests and diseases

As for brassicas (see pages 18, 19, 20, 22).

Storage and kitchen hints

For freezing use tender shoots and treat like cabbage (p. 20)

Kale can be harvested from DECEMBER to APRIL. Serve kale in butter with poached eggs.

KOHL RABI

How to grow

This tastes like a cross between a turnip and a cabbage.

Sow the seeds in shallow drills, 12 inches apart in MARCH to JULY. Thin to 8 inches when seedlings are large enough to handle.

Water well in dry weather as they must grow quickly to produce tender stems. Pull the roots when they are the size of a cricket ball.

Try the varieties 'White Vienna', 'Early Purple' and 'Early White'.

Pests and diseases

Prone to *cabbage root fly* and *club root*. Treatment is the same as for Cabbages (see pages 18 and 19).

For *root fly*, treat with bromophos dust, for *club root*, dip roots of young plants in paste based on calomel.

Storage and kitchen hints

Lift the plants, trim and store in sand in a box in a shed (see Carrots page 21).

LEEKS

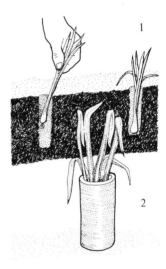

How to grow

They need a well manured soil to crop well, so can follow runner beans. Otherwise prepare the soil with manure or compost and leave rough dug over Winter.

Sow in seed boxes under glass FEBRUARY to MARCH or outdoors in APRIL. Plant out 9 inches apart in 6 inches deep dibber holes (1), 15 inches between rows, from JUNE onwards. DO NOT FILL HOLES – watering will do this.

Liquid feed once a fortnight, keep weed-free and earth up as they grow to get long white stems. Cardboard collars (2) or pipes will do as well (see Celery p. 23).

Try the varieties: 'Prizetaker' and 'Royal Favourite'.

Pests and diseases

Usually trouble free, but in very wet conditions *onion white rot* is a problem – treat with calomel dust.

Storage and kitchen hints

Leeks are hardy enough to leave in the soil over Winter. Try leek, potato and ham bone soup.

LETTUCE

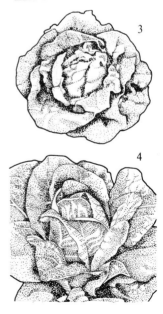

How to grow

In small gardens most economically used as an intercrop (see page 8). Requires a rich and fertile soil, manured and well dug the previous Autumn.

Sow seeds indoors in trays JANUARY and FEBRUARY. Prick out seedlings, then plant out in a cold frame or under cloches in MARCH. Plant or sow in the open ground from APRIL onwards. Sow at fortnightly intervals throughout the Summer. Leave thinning until they are large enough to eat. Then space the remainder 9 inches apart to heart up. Sow under cloches in mid-SEPTEMBER to overwinter.

Try the varieties: 'Unrivalled' (3) (cloche work), 'Tom Thumb' (Spring), and 'Lobjoits' (4) (Summer).

Pests and diseases

Greenfly – spray with liquid derris.

Grey mould – a problem on cold soil, also caused by damaging the seedlings while hoeing. Water with thiram.

Cover with black thread or cloches to keep birds off.

Storage and kitchen hints

Cannot be frozen.

Melons

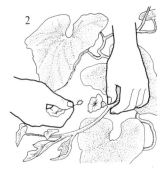

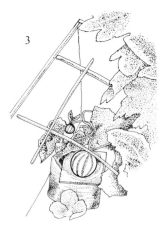

How to grow

Well worth the effort of growing. Their flavour wh
freshly cut is impossible to achieve with fruit bought i
shop. Warmth and moisture are essential, so grow und
glass.

Soil must be enriched with well rotted manure or compo
made up in ridges as for courgettes. Compost fill
polythene bags are very suitable for growing melons.

Sow 2 seeds indoors in APRIL in a peat pot. Aft
germination remove the weakest seedling, leaving th
strongest to be planted out in the prepared position in la
MAY.

Pinch out growing tip when each plant produces five leav
(1). As flowers appear, fertilise the female (identified b
small fruit behind the flower) with the male. Pick ma
flower, remove petals and place it onto the stigma of fema
flower to complete fertilization (2). Pollinate four fema
flowers at the same time. This ensures that all four fru
swell evenly. Fertilizing only one female flower preven
any subsequent fruit from developing. Increase waterir
and feeding once the small fruit have set.

As they swell, stand young fruits on a piece of glass or woc
to keep clear of soil (3). Allow only 4 fruit to each plant ar
give them all the sun available.

The fragrance from ripe fruit is unmistakable, but check t
pressing end furthest away from stalk. If it gives a little the
the fruit is ripe enough to eat.

Try the varieties: 'Ha-Ogen' (mini fruited); 'Honeyde
(greenhouse only); 'Hero of Lockinge' (for frames
'Charentais' (for frames).

Pests and diseases

Both *red spider* and *white fly* are encouraged by po
growing conditions. Damp overhead in hot weather bo
morning and evening.

Downy mildew is encouraged by over moist conditions,
ventilate when weather is bright and sunny.

Planting on a ridge prevents water collecting around th
stem – stops *stem rot*.

Storage and kitchen hints

It is better to pick fruit ripe from frame in warm sun, and e
straight away with no additives.

'Honeydew' and 'Cantaloup' are the best varieties f
freezing. Cut in two, then cut flesh into cubes, sprinkle wit
sugar and pack in polythene bags.

Mustard & Cress/Onions (Spring)

How to grow

An ideal vegetable for introducing children to gardening as it can be grown on a window sill.

Sow at ANY TIME. Grow in small trifle dishes or plastic trays with a piece of blotting paper in the bottom. Sow the cress in one container – mustard, which grows more quickly, three days later in another.

Keep in light warm position. Plants must be grown rapidly to ensure the leaves are tender. Always use luke warm water to keep the blotting paper moist. A growing temperature of 45 degrees F. is adequate. Cut when ready with scissors usually 11–14 days later. Sow a small amount each week.

Storage and kitchen hints

Try chopped with hard boiled eggs on chicory slices.

MUSTARD AND CRESS

How to grow

Grown as an intercrop with parsnips, peas or lettuce. Alternatively as a catch crop when ground falls vacant, for example after carrots. Work into the soil a dressing of fish meal – 3 oz/sq yard before sowing. Sow in drills $\frac{1}{4}$ inch deep from MARCH to JULY. For a continual supply sow in short rows 6 feet long at 6 week intervals. For overwintering sow 'White Lisbon' (Winter variety) in SEPTEMBER to crop the following APRIL.

Keep weed free and well watered. If some salad onions grow too big they can be left and used for pickling.

Try the varieties: 'White Lisbon' and 'Paris Silverskin' (for pickling).

ONIONS (SPRING)

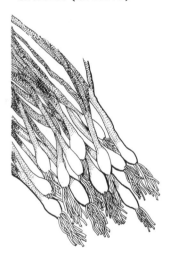

Pests and diseases

Onion fly – white maggots. To prevent, dust the rows with calomel before sowing.

White rot – white fungal growth. Burn any seedlings and dust row with calomel. Do not plant onions in same place next year.

Storage and kitchen hints

For pickling – peel onions and place in salt water (2 ozs/pt. water) and leave overnight. Remove, drain well, pack into jars and cover with spiced vinegar. Leave to stand for 8–12 weeks before use.

Try salad onions chopped with cod roe as a savoury omelette filling.

Onions

ONIONS

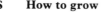

1

2

How to grow

Best grown in the same bed for several years to build up fertility.

Soil must be dug deeply with compost or manure incorporated in the Autumn. Rake down and firm to a fine level bed before sowing or planting.

Sow variety 'Ailsa Craig' in greenhouse in FEBRUARY under cloches in MARCH. Transplant in late APRIL when soil is warm. Seeds may be sown direct in rows 12 inches apart in drills $\frac{1}{4}$ inch deep in mid-APRIL. In cold districts, plant onion sets (small dry bulbs) in APRIL – push into soil so that only top is exposed – best if just rooted before planting in tray of moist peat so that the worms cannot pull them out.

Fresh manure will cause thick necked bulbs. Where Autumn cultivations are not possible, prepare the soil with fertilizer only – 3 ozs/sq yard.

Plant in rows 12 inches apart, 6 inches between bulbs.

If sown direct it's important to keep weeds down. Hand weed so as not to disturb roots. When large enough to use in salads, thin seedlings to leave plants 6 inches apart. Liquid feed in MAY and JUNE once every 14 days.

In AUGUST, when stems yellow, bend tops over into centre of row to help ripen up bulbs (2). Cloches over the rows also helps ripening. In late AUGUST lift bulbs to a dry, sunny, airy place, on glass in a half opened frame to complete drying process.

Try the varieties: 'Ailsa Craig', 'Bedfordshire Champion', 'Produrijn' and 'Stuttgarter Giant' (sets).

Pests and diseases

Onion fly – attracted by smell of damaged foliage. Lift and burn infected bulbs.

White rot or mouldy nose – fungal growth at base of bulb. Lift and burn infected bulbs. Grow onions on a different plot next year, and dust drills with calomel.

Neck rot – neck of bulb goes soft and brown. Examine bulbs in store frequently and remove diseased bulbs.

Storage and kitchen hints

Store in wire netting trays or, even better, rope in bunches (2) and hang in a cool, dry, airy place.

Small onions may be frozen whole – blanched for 4 minutes and used for cooking only. Large onions are peeled, chopped, packed and sealed in containers.

Parsnips

How to grow

These follow cabbage in the rotation.

Soil must be rough dug the previous Autumn with a little manure or compost incorporated. The deeper the soil can be worked the better the root development. Alternatively, work in 2 oz/sq yard of a phosphate/potash mixture when making down in the Spring. DO NOT grow on freshly manured ground as this causes forked roots.

Sow seed from MARCH to early MAY in drills ½ inch deep, 15 inches between rows. Parsnip seeds are slow to germinate, so mix with radish seed which comes up quickly to show the line of rows. This enables the weeds to be recognised and controlled. Pick the radish when mature.

Thin parsnip seedlings to 6 inches apart when tall enough to handle. Discard thinnings as they do not transplant. Hoe regularly between rows to keep weeds down.

Follow parsnips with potatoes in the rotation.

Try the varieties: 'Intermediate-White Gem' (a promising new intermediate variety); 'Tender and True' (long); 'Offenham' (short).

Use short or intermediate varieties on shallow soils.

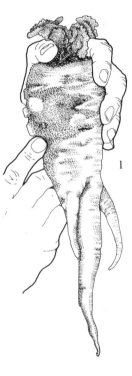

Pests and diseases

Canker – shows as rusty patches on skin (1) at first followed by internal rotting. Canker is associated with poor soil conditions and is caused by fungi. The risk of attack is reduced by adding lime and potash before sowing and by avoiding damaging the roots when weeding. Also practising crop rotation helps reduce this condition. On susceptible soils grow 'Tender and True'.

Leaf miner – larvae feed on leaf tissues. Adult flies lay eggs on underside of leaves, and larvae mine in the leaf tissue itself resulting in white marks on the surface. It can damage the leaf and reduce the yield. Control by spraying with malathion.

Storage and kitchen hints

Flavour is improved if roots are left in the soil until the first frost and used as required.

They are ready for lifting when the leaves begin to die in the late Autumn or early Winter. Roots can be lifted then stored in sand to clear land for digging. (see carrots page 31).

For freezing, peel young parsnips and cut into strips. Blanch for 2 minutes, cool, dry and pack.

Peas

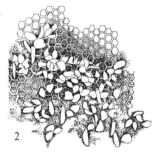

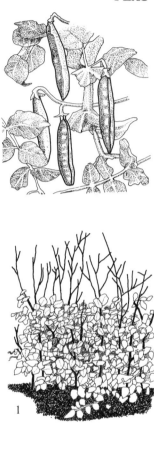

PEAS

How to grow

Need a well manured, deeply worked, weed free soil. Ca
follow potatoes or, failing this, the land should be dug an
well manured the previous Autumn. Where manure is i
short supply, take out a trench 12 inches wide and 14 inche
deep. Put a layer of manure or compost into it. Refill t
within 3 inches of the top. It is often possible, however, t
grow a good crop from ground which is newly broken i
from old grassland.

Sow the seed in shallow trenches 2–3 inches deep and
inches wide in APRIL to JUNE. 3 or 4 rows of peas to eac
trench, spaced 2–3 inches each way. The spacing betwee
varieties can differ but even with tall growing peas
providing they are staked up, you never need more than 2
inches between each row even in a small garden. Sow at 1
day intervals for harvesting from JULY to SEPTEMBER.

Keep the weeds down. Stake the rows when seedlings are
inches high with twiggy branches (1). Plastic netting place
along the outside of the rows can also be used as support (2)
Water in dry weather to help pods fill. Mulching betwee
rows with compost prevents the soil being beaten dow
hard.

Try the varieties: 'Pilot', 'Early Onward', 'Feltham First'
(earlies); 'Greenshaft', 'Kelvedon Wonder' (maincrop).

Pests and diseases

Mildew – white powdery substance. Usually occurs durin
mid-Summer. Later sowings should be protected b
sulphur dust. Keep the garden clear of weeds and cro
debris.

Foot rot – rotting of stems caused by a poorly drained soil

Thrips – tiny insects which tear holes in leaves. Damp th
rows over in the evening and spray with liquid derris.

Pea moth – this lays eggs on the flowers which produc
maggots. Avoid by sowing early maturing varieties fo
picking by mid-JULY; sow late varieties after mid-JUNE.

Sparrows eat the young shoots, so cover with netting o
cotton.

Storage and kitchen hints

Pick the pods while young and tender. Those which harde
can be dried and made into soup.

An ideal vegetable for freezing but only use young, swee
green peas. Shell and blanch for 1 minute. Cool, drain an
pack in polythene bags.

How to grow

They really are very easy to grow. A sunny warm position outdoors or a greenhouse in cold areas is ideal. May be grown as a kitchen window sill plant or as a patio plant.

Peppers need a light, fertile, well drained soil enriched with rotted compost or manure. Given a well prepared soil and reasonable shelter from cold winds, a crop of peppers can be grown in most areas of the country outdoors.

Sow seeds in APRIL, prick off seedlings when 2 leaves have unfurled into peat pots. Plant out into compost filled polythene bags, pots or direct into greenhouse border. Outdoors, sow under glass in late APRIL and plant out in early JUNE.

Water freely, syringe overhead in dry weather to help set the fruit. Green peppers are the immature fruit picked before they turn red. A plant potted up and grown on a window sill will produce peppers from JULY to SEPTEMBER.

Don't leave green peppers on the plant to go red as this will reduce the total crop.

Liquid feed every 10 days once the fruits start to swell.

Pests and diseases

Capsid bug – feeds on growing tips and can weaken the plant. Check by spraying with derris pyrethrum.

Storage and kitchen hints

Peppers can be frozen – but red and green must be frozen separately. Cut in half (1), wash, remove stems and seeds. Then blanch for 3 minutes in halves for stuffing, in slices for stewing. Cool, drain and pack.

PEPPERS

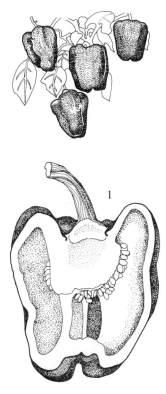

1

How to grow

The best crop for cleaning and improving rough land. Dig in well rotted manure in the Autumn. If the soil is clay, leave it in rough clods to weather. Light soils can be dug, manured and planted at one and the same time in the spring.

Stand the 'sets' (tubers) for planting upright on a light cool window sill to grow short green sprouts (shoots) (2) during early MARCH. Plant 'earlies' in APRIL 15 inches apart, 18 inches between rows. Plant main crop later in the month 15 inches apart, 24 inches between rows. All 4 inches to 5 inches deep.

POTATOES

2

Potatoes (continued)

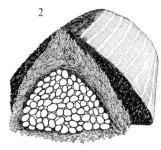

A dusting of fertilizer in the hole at planting time increas[e]
the crop. Earth up (raising soil up around plants so they a[re]
covered more deeply than at soil level) as growth proceed[s].
This protects the tubers and prevents them from turni[ng]
green, resulting in a bitter taste.

Instead of planting the tubers, useful crops of potatoes m[ay]
be grown by using sheets of black polythene as a cove[r].
Prepare the soil as previously described, roll out t[he]
polythene, and cut holes at 15 inch spacings. Plant t[he]
tubers by pushing them into the soft soil through the[se]
holes. The polythene is anchored securely by throwi[ng]
some soil on the loose edges so that no wind can get unde[r].
Once the potato leaves develop, the sheeting is very firm[ly]
held. Potatoes are harvested by lifting the black polythe[ne]
carefully from one edge, removing the tubers which a[re]
large enough (1). Replace the polythene until remainin[g]
tubers develop. The tops of earlies (not under polythen[e])
should be covered when the frost threatens. Earth up [as]
growth proceeds.

Harvesting (not under polythene) – lift early crop [as]
required. Main crop for storing in OCTOBER.

Try the varieties: 'Home Guard', 'Ulster Chieftai[n]'
(earlies); 'Majestic', 'Pentland Dell' (maincrop).

Pests and diseases

Wire worm – found on newly cultivated grassland so gr[ow]
only early varieties.

Eel worm – microscopic in size but can reduce the crop [by]
half so practise a long rotation.

Blight – spray in suspect areas with zineb or Bordea[ux]
mixture. Cut and burn tops before lifting crop.

Wart – uncommon but must be reported to the Ministry [of]
Agriculture and all infected tubers burnt.

Storage and kitchen hints

When lifting in early OCTOBER take care not to damage t[he]
tubers. Allow 2 hours to dry. Store in a potato clamp (2[).]
Cover potatoes first with straw and then with a layer of s[oil]
to keep out the frost. Make sure the straw pokes through t[he]
top. This allows ventilation to take place.

Can be frozen but have to be partially cooked or fried first[;]
blanching time 3 minutes.

Try cooking clean new potatoes whole with mint. Ne[w]
potatoes cooked, dipped in salt and butter with a glass [of]
cold milk makes a grand supper.

Radishes/Rhubarb

RADISHES

How to grow

A catch, or intercrop, salad vegetable which can be grown in short rows and is quick maturing. They really are very easy to grow. The richer, more fertile the soil the better. Work soil to a fine tilth.

Sow from mid-MARCH onwards at 3 week intervals. Stop sowing in mid-MAY, radishes are not a Summer crop. Ideal for early salads if sown in frames or under cloches. Can be sown as early as mid-JANUARY and as late as SEPTEMBER. If a very early crop is required, choose the most sheltered corner of the garden. Cover the soil with sand, scatter the radish seed, rake in, and cover with black polythene or straw until seedlings germinate. Control weeds and water well in dry periods.

Try the varieties: 'Cherry Belle', 'French Breakfast' and the long rooted 'Icicle'.

Try them eaten straight from the garden with crisp, home made, wholemeal bread.

Pests and diseases

Leaves of seedlings may be attacked by larvae of *flea beetle*. Control by spraying with liquid derris.

RHUBARB

How to grow

Not strictly a vegetable but useful to have at one end of the plot. It needs a rich, fertile soil with plenty of rotted manure worked into the top 18 inches. Plant crown roots obtainable from garden shops in early MARCH, 2 feet apart and keep well watered. Mulch with rotted manure or compost. Liquid feed when growth begins in Spring with high nitrogen fertilizer. DO NOT gather rhubarb in the first season. Force in Winter by lifting roots in NOVEMBER to DECEMBER and planting them in soil and peat in a warm dark place. Plants can be forced outdoors by covering selected crowns with e.g. buckets (1), frames (2) – anything which keeps the plants dark and warm.

Pests and diseases

Usually none to worry about but *black bean aphids* feed on the young shoots. Spray with liquid derris.

Storage and kitchen hints

Pick sticks while young. Cut, trim and place in a polythene bag and freeze.

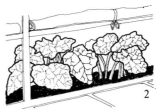

Shallots/Spinach

SHALLOTS

How to grow

Best grown in the same place for several years. Dig so deeply with manure or compost incorporated in the previous Autumn. Allow to settle, rake down and firm before planting unless weather is very wet.

Plant bulbs late FEBRUARY–MARCH 6 inches apart and 1 inches between rows. Press firmly into the soil so the top is showing (1). Replant those the worms pull out until root develop enough to prevent displacement.

Keep the weeds down by hand picking so as not to disturb roots. Apply 1 nitrogenous liquid feed in mid-APRIL.

Try varieties: 'Dutch Yellow' or 'Giant Yellow' or from seed 'Giant Red'.

Pests and diseases

Onion fly – as with onions lift and burn infected bulbs. The pest may be checked by spraying with a dilute solution of trichlorophon around the plants in MAY.

White rot – mouldy bulbs. Lift and burn infected bulbs and dust rows with calomel at planting time. Grow shallots on different plot next year.

Storage and kitchen hints

Lift bunches of bulbs and leave them under cloches or on path to dry. Clean, sort and store in a frost free shed.

SPINACH

How to grow

A fertile, moisture retentive soil ensures a continuous supply of tender leaves. Dig the soil a single spit deep (10–12 inches). Add well rotted manure or compost during the Winter.

Sow Summer spinach in drills 1 inch deep and rows 12 inches apart from MARCH to JULY. Thin seedlings to 6 inches apart. Can be sown at 6–8 week intervals as required. Mid-Summer sowings should be sited in the shade of taller growing crops to prevent early seeding.

Keep well watered in dry weather.

Sow Winter spinach mid-JULY to SEPTEMBER in a sheltered sunny spot. Thin seedlings to 6 inches apart and from OCTOBER onwards protect with cloches or straw between rows.

Try the varieties: 'Greenmarket' (Winter); 'Sigmaleaf' (dual purpose); 'Long Standing Round' (Summer).

Spinach/Spinach Beet/Swedes

sts and diseases

ildew – on underside of leaves shows as yellow blotches on
top. Spray with Bordeaux mixture or zineb.

llowing of leaves caused by *spinach blight*. Destroy leaves
burning.

ack fly – spray with liquid derris.

orage and kitchen hints

n be frozen successfully by selecting young leaves. Wash
ll and drain. Blanch for 2 minutes in small amounts, cool
d press out excess moisture. Pack in polythene bags
ving 1 inch headspace.

ow to grow

g soil single spit deep (12–14 inches) with well rotted
mpost added previous Autumn. Sow seed 1 inch deep
d 15 inches apart from APRIL to JULY. Thin seedlings to 6
ches apart, and liquid feed at 3 week intervals.

eep well watered in dry weather. Use the young leaves for
ting and remove old foliage to encourage young growth.
ook and eat young leaves as for spinach.

ests and diseases

sually no problems.

SPINACH BEET

ow to grow

winter vegetable which follows peas and beans in the
tation. It needs a soil well manured for a previous crop.
vedes do not grow well in acid soil so add 6 oz/sq yard of
ne 2–3 weeks before sowing. Sow seeds APRIL to MAY in
ills ½ inch deep. Thin seedlings to 6 inches apart.

ave roots in the ground until Christmas if no severe frost.

ry the variety 'Chignecto'.

ests and diseases

ember of the cabbage family (brassica) so susceptible to
bbage root fly and *club root* of cabbage. To prevent the *fly*,
st with bromophos dust. Only grow in same place every
ur years. (see pages 18, 19, 20, 22).

SWEDES

torage and kitchen hints

ore roots in sacks or under straw in a frost free place.

Sweetcorn

SWEETCORN

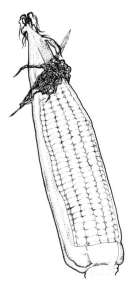

How to grow

Needs shelter, warmth and all the sunshine possible. In wet season the crop can be reduced by 50 per cent on poor drained soil. In the rotation this follows Spring cabbage. Dig in well rotted manure or compost, rake in a dressing fertilizer 3 oz/sq yard 10 days before sowing or planting.

In the North sow under glass during mid-APRIL for planting outside late MAY. Sow 2 seeds to a peat pot – remove weakest after germination. Plant out 15 inches apart 24 inches between rows. In the open ground sow 2 seeds to each position 15 inches apart 24 inches between rows. Remove the weakest seedlings after germination.

To provide shelter, plant behind a row of runner beans. Plant in blocks, 3 rows wide at least, to ensure the pollen from the male flowers (at the top of the plant) is carried by the wind to all female flowers (between stem and leaves) (This ensures the cobs fill evenly. Tapping the male flowers lightly when in full bloom, JUNE–JULY, helps spread the pollen.

Water heavily in dry weather. A mulch of compost down the row also conserves moisture. Sweetcorn is difficult to grow in the North unless the Summer is very warm.

Try the variety 'First of All'.

Pests and diseases

Usually no problems especially with pot raised plants. Birds may strip the tips of the cob – drape nets over the plants.

Storage and kitchen hints

Sweetcorn is usually harvested from early AUGUST to mid OCTOBER. The cobs are ripe when the silk tassle at the ear dry and brown with the cob well filled to hand. Also check by easing leaves of cob back to see if grains of corn are ripe. When pressing with a finger nail they should, if ripe, ooze milky liquid. Snap the cobs from the stem and eat immediately.

An ideal vegetable for freezing. Remove husks and silk. Blanch for 4–8 minutes depending on size, cool and dry. Pack singly in foil.

To cook, place cobs in a pan of unsalted water and boil for 15–20 minutes. Drain and serve with melted butter, salt and pepper to taste.

For corn fritters – make a batter up from 4oz flour, an egg, pint of milk and salt to taste. Add 6oz of thawed-out kernels and fry spoonfuls until crisp.

How to grow

TOMATOES

These need a greenhouse, or a warm sheltered site if grown outdoors, if the fruit are to ripen.

Change the soil in a greenhouse every year to reduce the risk of root disease. Plants can be grown in rings (bottomless pots filled with compost) standing on a 4 inch deep layer of ash or gravel (1). Providing the ash and gravel is sterilised, it can be used for several years. Large polythene bags filled with a peat based compost can also be used (2). When tomatoes are grown in containers, make sure the compost is always moist.

Outdoors choose a sheltered position in full sun. Dig in well-rotted manure and ten days before planting rake in 3 oz of tomato fertilizer per sq yard.

Sow seed for indoor plants in FEBRUARY, for outdoor varieties in early APRIL under glass. Sow 2 seeds in a peat pot, remove the weakest after germination. A warm light place e.g. a window sill, is ideal for young plants before planting outside. Harden off (getting plants used to outside conditions) and plant outside in late MAY, 18 inches apart and 24 inches between rows.

Indoor and outdoor plants must have no check to growth, so avoid draughts or cold winds. Support growing plants with a cane or string so that developing fruits are kept well clear of the soil.

Remove the small shoots which appear in the axil (where the leaf joins the stem) unless an outdoors bush variety is being grown, when they are left to produce fruit. Tap the supports daily (about midday) to help pollination. Syringe over the plants with water afterwards. A layer of peat, straw or any organic material (mulch) helps to conserve moisture. Commence liquid feeding when the fruit on the bottom truss are the size of peas, and continue at 10 day intervals. When 7 trusses have set, outdoors 4, pinch out the growing tip to encourage fruit to ripen up.

Try the varieties: 'Moneymaker', 'Golden Queen', 'Ailsa Craig', (indoors); 'French Cross', 'Sleaford Abundance' (outdoors).

Pests and diseases

Blossom end rot – shows as hard patches on the base of the fruit (3). Caused by a shortage of water at some stage in the plant's growth. Keep the moisture supply constant.

Foot and root rot – too much water due to bad drainage. Make sure soil is in good condition, and in the greenhouse change it each year.

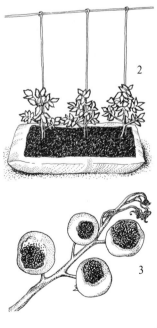

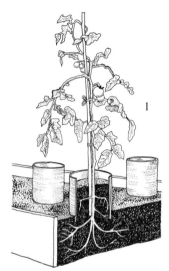

Green back – hard green patches on stalk end of fruit which fails to ripen, due to potash deficiency or excess sunlight. Feed with a high proportion of potash. Do not defoliate too much and shade on very hot days.

Grey mould – (fungus growth) and *leaf mould* (yellow blotches on upper sides of leaves) (1). Usually only trouble some in wet seasons or with poor ventilation or when over crowded. Wounds left by careless side shooting may also help the fungus gain a hold. Improve ventilation and air circulation, keep the humidity lower.

Potato blight (2) – usually only a problem on outdoor tomatoes. Spray with a liquid copper spray or zineb after early AUGUST at 3 week intervals.

White fly – common in greenhouses. Spray with malathion.

Storage and kitchen hints

Pick fruits as they ripen. Fruit still green at end of season will ripen if picked and wrapped in soft paper and stored in a dark, warm airy place. They will also ripen on a kitchen window sill. At the first frost remove whole plant and supporting cane and hang upside down in a frost-free shed. Green tomatoes can be made into chutney.

Freeze ripe tomatoes for purée. Skin, then core tomatoes and simmer for 5 minutes until soft. Pass through a nylon sieve, cool, pack in small sealed polythene boxes.

TURNIPS

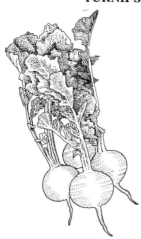

How to grow

Follow beans in rotation but can be used as a successional crop after leeks. Fork in lightly a high phosphate fertilizer at 2 oz/sq yard 10 days before sowing. Sow seeds in drills ½ inch deep, 12 inches apart from APRIL to mid-JULY. Thin seedlings to 6 inches apart. Water in dry weather.

Try the varieties: 'Purple and White Milan' and 'Golden Ball'.

Pests and diseases

Flea beetles – water well after dusk.

Storage and kitchen hints

Store in sand and keep in a frost free shed.

For freezing, use small turnips, trim and cut into small slices. Blanch for 2½ minutes, cool, drain and pack in sealed, rigid polythene boxes.

Monthly calendar of work

This gardening calendar is an average for the country – in warmer areas a fortnight earlier, and in exposed areas 2–3 weeks later.

JANUARY

Cultivation

Complete the Winter digging – leave clods rough for the frost to break down.

Prepare compost for seed sowing. Scrub down greenhouse with disinfectant. Order vegetable seed.

Plant rhubarb roots 2 feet apart. (Can be obtained from garden shops.)

Vegetables in Season

Brussels sprouts, cabbage, savoys, artichokes (Jerusalem), leeks, parsnips, chicory, celery, kale – from the open garden.

Vegetables in Store

Potatoes, carrots, beetroot, onions, shallots, garlic, turnips, swedes.

FEBRUARY

Cultivation

Dress plot intended for cabbages, cauliflowers, sprouts and broccoli with lime once the digging is completed.

Clear all plant debris to the compost heap as the crops are removed.

Sow early lettuce, cabbage, onions (salad), carrots under cloches, cauliflowers in a heated frame.

Continue to pick sprouts starting with the bottom buttons and remove the foliage as the picking proceeds up the stem.

Order asparagus plants and dig site.

Store parsnips in sand on a North wall to prevent them starting into growth.

Vegetables in Season

As for JANUARY.

MARCH

Cultivation

Stand seed potatoes, shoot end uppermost in trays to start sprouting. Choose a light, cool but frost-free airy place so the shoots grow strong and sturdy.

Dig the land occupied by overwintering crops as it comes vacant. Do not forget this land will carry roots, so a fortnight before sowing dress the soil with superphosphate and sulphate of potash.

Harden off Autumn-sown cauliflowers.

Sow small salads – radish, mustard and cress for succession.

Plant shallots.

Sow broad beans, spinach, early peas, cabbage, sprouts, parsley, onions, carrots and early tomatoes.

Lift remaining leeks to free the ground and heel them in under a North wall to check growth.

Side dress Spring cabbage with a quick-acting nitrogenous fertilizer (nitrate of soda) to encourage leaf growth.

Vegetables in Season

Late Brussels sprouts, broccoli, spring greens, chicory, kale, early salads from frames. Onions and carrots from store.

APRIL

Cultivation

Complete the hardening off of plants in frames – lettuce, onions, cauliflowers.

Prick off seedlings as they get to the first true leaf stage. Sow later in the month under glass, runner beans, melons, courgettes, marrows and cucumbers.

Sow outdoors – peas, broad beans, cabbage, cauliflowers, Brussels sprouts, onions, salads, beetroot (late in the month), spinach, parsnips, chicory.

Pot on tomatoes sown last month.

Monthly calendar of work

Prepare a trench for both runner beans and celery.

Overgrown herbs such as mint and chives may be lifted, divided and replanted.

Sow parsley in short rows to follow the crop grown under cloches.

Plant potatoes in well prepared soil.

Clear Brussels sprouts from the land and burn old stumps.

Keep the push hoe at work between rows of germinating seeds to reduce weeding later.

Vegetables in Season

As for MARCH.

MAY

Cultivation

Sow sweet corn, runner beans, marrows under cloches early in the month.

Outdoors – maincrop peas, French beans, savoys, also beetroot salads and spinach as successional crops.

Stake early peas.

Cut shoots from asparagus plants over 2 years old.

Thin early sowings of beetroot, lettuce, cauliflowers.

Protect tops of early potatoes from late frost by drawing a little soil over them on cold nights.

Mulch between the rows of peas and beans with compost.

Dig the ground cleared of sprouting broccoli, dress with potash and superphosphate before sowing maincrop carrots, beetroot and parsnips.

Start a compost heap with all the debris, weeds, thinnings, kitchen (vegetable) waste.

Vegetables in Season

Winter cauliflower, sprouting broccoli, kale, early salads.

Pests and diseases

Keep a careful watch for blackfly on broad beans, flea beetle and cabbage root fly (cabbage plants wilting under bright sun is an indication of maggots feeding on the roots).

Extra care should be taken to provide protection in case of late frost.

On newly broken-in land, watch for wireworm damage on early lettuce (plant wilting).

JUNE

Cultivation

There should be little fear of late frost by this time, so all the tender plants can go out at the end of the first week. Protect from cold winds with cloches, polythene or hessian screens.

Plant out cauliflowers, cabbage, early sprouts, marrows, courgettes, tomatoes.

Stake the runner beans.

Remove the tops from early broad beans as pods set to lessen the risk of blackfly attack.

Sow peas and salads for succession, Summer spinach, beetroot, carrots, sweet corn, garden swedes.

Thin early sowings as required.

Hoe between all the crops – except onions which later in the month need hand weeding. Liquid feed onions, root crops and cauliflowers.

Vegetable in Season

Broad beans – tips and immature pods (edible), spinach, carrots, radish, salads, cauliflowers (overwintered in frame).

Pests and diseases

Watch out for thrip on peas (spray with liquid derris), cabbage root fly on cabbage, sprouts and cauliflowers. Onion fly and greenfly apply insecticides. Slug pellets for runner beans – remember, these are poisonous to children and pets, so cover.